pray

21 Days of Guided Prayer to Ignite Your Prayer Life and Grow Closer to God

Kathryn Shirey

Dedication

This prayer journal is dedicated to the women of the Nocona "Be Still" conference and the St. Philip's "Be Still" retreat who graciously allowed me to lead them through many of these prayer methods. I was overwhelmed watching the Holy Spirit move through the room and touch your hearts. My prayer is for the Holy Spirit to similarly touch and move each person who embarks on this 21 day journey through prayer.

A special thank you to my husband Larry for supporting me in this writing endeavor. Thank you also to Kelley and Tracie who have been so instrumental in providing guidance and support to my journey. Thank you for the laughs, the long lunches, and the clarity you brought to *Pray Deep* as we developed "Be Still."

Stir up your power, O Lord, and with great might come among us; and, because we are sorely hindered by our sins, let your bountiful grace and mercy speedily help and deliver us; through Jesus Christ our Lord, to whom, with you and the Holy Spirit, be honor and glory, now and forever. Amen.

(Collect for the Third Sunday of Advent, page 212, The Book of Common Prayer)

Table of Contents

INTRODUCTION TO PRAYING DEEP

What is your definition of prayer? Is it the bedtime prayers of your childhood, kneeling beside your bed asking God's blessing over a list of your family and friends? Is it the prayers you hear in church, seeming somehow out of reach and poetic, as if only a prayer expert can say them? Is it a request you see sent out over email or Facebook, asking for prayers of healing or strength through a tough time? Or could it be something more meaningful and integral in your life?

At its core, prayer is our conversation with God. It's all of the things above – and more. So often, though, we think of conversation as our words. Yet prayer is more than words. Having a candid, extemporaneous conversation {prayer} with God is wonderful, but have you considered other ways to connect with God?

Praying Deep: Ignite Your Prayer Life

Praying Deep is about exploring different ways to pray, using varied techniques and approaches to build a deeper, more meaningful relationship with God. We're each created unique, with different learning styles and preferred senses, so why wouldn't God want to connect with us in the way He's wired us? Prayer can be experienced through music, written words, art, movement, and silent listening, just to name a few.

I've discovered that developing a varied approach to prayer and exploring deeper ways to pray has ignited my prayer life, making prayer a more profound and powerful experience. I've developed more consistent prayer habits and grown closer to God. Through the Pray Deep series of prayer journals, I want to share this approach with you and help you also ignite your prayer life and grow closer to God.

What To Expect

In this first *Pray Deep* 21-day prayer journal, we'll explore the basics of prayer and beyond, introducing you to almost 20 different techniques for praying and connecting with God. Some will be familiar, others may be new to you. Some may feel uncomfortable, but I encourage you to give them a try and see for yourself how you can connect with God on an even deeper level.

Will you join me in learning to Pray Deep? Try out these prayer techniques, especially if they're new or unfamiliar. Give them a chance and see which ones you like the best. Then, add them into your prayer routine. Ignite your own prayer life and see how you can connect to God more deeply.

How To Use This Prayer Journal

Plan to set aside at least 20-30 minutes each day to complete the reading and prayers. Each day will include an introduction to a prayer topic and then guide you through prayer utilizing that particular technique. You will have space to take notes and journal about your experience.

PRAYER AS CONVERSATION

As our small group meeting was ending, the leader asked if anyone would close us in prayer. Instinctively, I buried my head in my Bible, trying not to make eye contact, hoping desperately one of the "good pray-ers" would volunteer. You know, the ones who always sound so eloquent and seem to have the perfect words. I squirmed a little in my chair, feeling my face become flushed, as the leader looked for someone to ask.

Have you ever felt this way? Why are we so afraid to pray in public? Why are we so uncertain even in our private prayer time?

I used to think prayers had to be said a certain way or use special poetic language. The prayers I always heard at church were so beautifully written. I didn't always understand them, but loved how they sounded. However, I could never get my prayers to sound quite the same. I got frustrated and felt that my prayers weren't good enough or weren't the right words to take to God.

Then I learned prayer is simply a conversation with God and He wants to talk with us in whatever words we can muster, even when we can't even find the words to say. We don't have to follow a set script or formula. We don't have to use any specific words or poetic phrases. We only need to be present and start a dialog.

Let's look at some key elements of a good conversation and see how we can apply these to prayer. I don't always get each of these incorporated into my prayer. Sometimes my prayer will focus on just one or two, but I do try to touch on each throughout the day.

1) Start with a compliment or praise

Who doesn't like to hear something nice? We all love when a friend says something nice - compliments our hair or shoes, praises something we've done. God's no different. He loves to hear us praise Him.

God, you are amazing! What an awesome sunrise you created this morning.

2) Say thank you

We drill this into our children all the time to say 'thank you' anytime someone gives you something. It's a common curtesy and makes the other person feel appreciated and more willing to give again.

Thank you, God, for the blessings You pour down upon us. Thank you for bringing us together this day, to read and study Your word, and to learn how to have better conversations with You.

3) Share something about your day, what's going on in your life

God wants to be part of your life. To truly let Him in, you need to share what's happening in your life, what's on your heart. Maybe a concern you have from the day. Maybe a decision you need to make. Maybe something that's causing you stress and worry. What would you share if you were having this conversation with a friend?

God, sometimes I struggle with prayer. I know I should feel more comfortable talking to You and I should volunteer more to lead our group in prayer, but I just don't feel I'll have the right words.

4) Apologize for anything you've done

What is the other phrase we constantly drill into our children? "I'm sorry." We are forever guiding our kids to say "I'm sorry" when they've done anything wrong to someone else, yet we don't always set the best example, do we? How many times each day do we mess up? How often do we sin in thought, word, or deed? God wants to hear our "I'm sorry."

I'm sorry for not trusting You to guide me and help me find the words. Sorry for not believing You want to hear whatever words I have. I know prayer is not a contest for who has the best words, but instead is an offering of ourselves to You.

5) Make your requests - ask for yourself and others

Asking for ourselves and others is an essential part of prayer. This is where prayer can be so powerful and effective. Pour out your heart to God, asking Him for help, guidance, and healing. Pray for yourself and pray for others.

Lord, help me be more confident in my prayers so I can be a stronger leader. Help me boldly pray for myself and others, and then truly believe You are at work in these requests. When I can't find the right words, I trust You know even the groanings of my heart.

6) Listen

Finally, listen for God. Don't fill all your prayer time with your own words. If you were talking to someone in person, you'd give them a chance to talk, right? So, allow God the same space. You may not always hear Him in that moment, but be sure you build those quiet listening times into your life so you can hear God.

{Be quiet, take a deep breath, quiet your inner monologue, and then just sit in the silence and allow your soul to listen for God's response.}

GUIDE FOR PRAYING DEEP TODAY:

Now it's your turn. Take time today to re-introduce yourself to God. Start a conversation, or continue one you've already begun. Spend time in each of the six key elements of conversation. Don't worry if it feels awkward at first. Most conversations are until you really get to know someone. Lined pages are provided if you want to write your conversation or journal about the experience.

1) Start with a compliment or praise.

2) Say thank you.

3) Share something about your day.

4) Apologize for anything you've done (or not done).

5) Make your requests - for yourself and others.

6) Listen for God's response.

_____

_____

_____

_____

_____

_____

_____

_____

_____

_____

_____

_____

_____

_____

_____

_____

Almighty God, give us grace to cast away the works of darkness, and put on the armor of light, now in the time of this mortal life in which your Son Jesus Christ came to visit us in great humility; that in the last day, when he shall come again in his glorious majesty to judge both the living and the dead, we may rise to the life immortal; through him who lives and reigns with you and the Holy Spirit, one God, now and for ever. Amen.

(Collect for the First Sunday of Advent, page 211, The Book of Common Prayer)

PRAYER JOURNALING

It was a small, rectangular wooden box that caught his attention as we were cleaning out the closet. That heart-wrenching job you have to do after a loved one dies. Sorting through clothes, shoes, and intimate keepsakes with all the tender memories each item recalls. Yet, it was this box I'd never noticed before that caused new tears to well up in my dad's eyes.

He said it was full of letters. Love letters between the two of them sent while he was off at his first year of college and she was back home finishing high school. Letters she'd saved for nearly 50 years.

There's just something about the written word. I have my own collection of letters from my mother that I treasure - both the hand-written ones and the ones she typed when her handwriting began to deteriorate. I love seeing her words to me; words she took the time to write.

Write your prayers as a letter to God.

Just as we write letters to each other, we can also write letters to God. As you pray, try writing your prayers in a journal.

Some days words flow out my fingers faster than my mind can process and I am more free to share my heart with God through my writing. By keeping my prayers in a journal, I can also see how my prayers are changing and growing over time; even look back and see how God has been at work answering my prayers.

Keep track of prayer requests and answered prayers.

What do you do when someone asks for prayer? Maybe you stop and pray right then or pray the next time you think of that person, but do you keep praying continuously until the prayer is answered?

I've found it helps to keep a prayer request list in my prayer journal. Sometimes it's just a name and other times I'll write down something about the prayer need. As I pray, I'll pull out my list and pray for the names I've written down. If a prayer has been answered, I'll note that, too, and praise God for His great goodness.

Write down God's words to you.

As you pray or read scripture, God may place words on your heart. Maybe a Bible verse jumped off the page at you. What a friend calls a "flashing neon Bible verse." Or, maybe it's words or a picture you get while in prayer. Even a specific nudge you feel as you go through your day.

Keep track of these in your journal. Write down what you think God is trying to tell you. Look back over your journal and see what themes emerge. These messages from God are the most precious words I treasure in my heart and I don't want to forget or miss what He's telling me.

Maybe even write His words in a different color in your journal. One color for your thoughts and prayers, with another color for God's responses.

If prayers are our conversations with God, then journaling prayer is like writing Him love notes.

Find a journal today and get started.

I use a small one that fits in my purse, so it's always with me. You don't need anything expensive or special - just whatever you can find. A small spiral notebook from the school supply section at the dollar store or a small journal from the checkout line at Hobby Lobby will do.

- Just start writing each day.

- Write out a prayer.

- Write down which prayer method you tried that day and if you connected with it or not.

- Start a list of prayer requests to pray over.

- As God speaks to you, write down how you heard Him - a specific verse from the Bible, a nudge to do something, words or an image placed on your heart.

- As you try different prayer methods and techniques, journal about your experience.

> *"For prayer is nothing more than being on terms of friendship with God."*
>
> *~ St. Francis of Avala*

GUIDE FOR PRAYING DEEP TODAY:

Each day you'll have an opportunity to journal your prayers and your prayer experience. Start today by writing a letter to God. Is there something from yesterday's prayer that stood out to you? If so, go deeper and write God a letter about it.

O God, the strength of all who put their trust in you:
Mercifully accept our prayers; and because in our weakness
we can do nothing good without you, give us the help of
your grace, that in keeping your commandments we may
please you both in will and deed; through Jesus Christ our
Lord, who lives and reigns with you and the Holy Spirit, one
God, for ever and ever. Amen.

(Collect for the Sixth Sunday after the Epiphany, page 216,
The Book of Common Prayer)

praying the BOOK OF common prayer

I still remember that eye-opening moment in Senior English class as I waded through the required Shakespeare reading. That moment when I realized how Shakespeare's writing has become interwoven in our language today. His works are not just great works of historical literature, but part of the fabric of our lives today.

Just look at a few of the common phrases written by Shakespeare which we still use today: a laughing stock, eaten out of house and home, in a pickle, in the twinkling of an eye, send him packing, there's method in my madness, too much of a good thing, vanish into thin air.

What is the Book of Common Prayer?

Did you know the Book of Common Prayer (BCP) similarly has greatly influenced our language today? This book was originally compiled by Thomas Cranmer, the Archbishop of Canterbury under the reign of King Henry VIII as part of the reformation, but was also one of the first translations of the Litany and prayers into English.

If you said "till death do us part" at your wedding or expect the words "earth to earth, ashes to ashes, dust to dust" to be said at your funeral, then you have felt the impact of the Book of Common Prayer.

The prayers (or collects) are largely still based on Cranmer's translations from the Latin prayers. These centuries-old prayers are beautiful, lyrical, and powerful.

Why pray pre-written, formal prayers?

These are prayers that have held relevance for worshipers for centuries, so why wouldn't they still speak to us today? The rich language of these prayers can put you in a more reverent state to address our Almighty God. These prayers address timeless themes and needs.

I'm not Anglican, is the Book of Common Prayer applicable to me?

While the Book of Common Prayer is the basis for Anglican and Episcopal traditions, you'll find the prayers throughout a number of Christian traditions, often in their original form. John Wesley, the founder of Methodism, stated "I believe there is no Liturgy in the world, either in ancient or modern language, which breathes more of a solid, scriptural, rational piety than the Common Prayer of the Church of England."

Praying from the Book of Common Prayer

Try incorporating some of these prayers into your prayer life. Embrace the beauty of the language. Feel the power of a prayer that has been prayed for hundreds of years by millions of Christians.

1) Find The Book of Common Prayer.

The Book of Common Prayer is available online (http://www.bcponline.org) or you can purchase a hard copy. There are also several apps that will bring the BCP to your phone or iPad.

2) Look up the Collect (prayer) for the week and pray it.

This prayer will be prayed in churches across the world that Sunday, so you can join your voice with millions of others praying the same prayer that week.

3) Look up a Collect for a special purpose.

Whatever your need, you should be able to find an applicable prayer.

4) Write down your favorite prayers and pray them regularly.

I have several written out on index cards and I'll rotate through them as part of my daily prayer. Some are related to specific prayer needs and others are just prayers I found particularly beautiful or meaningful.

GUIDE FOR PRAYING DEEP TODAY:

Each day I'll provide a prayer from *The Book of Common Prayer* for you to use to close your prayer time. Read slowly, read aloud, soak in the words.

Today, pray the collect (prayer) below. Circle or underline the words that speak to you. Write your own prayer, putting it into your own words, focusing on the words or phrases that called to your heart.

Journal about your experience praying this ancient prayer. How do these words still apply to your life today? How does it feel to pray a pre-written prayer?

Almighty and everlasting God,
you are always more ready to hear
than we to pray,
and to give more than
we either desire or deserve:
Pour upon us the abundance of your mercy,
forgiving us those things
of which our conscience is afraid,
and giving us those good things
for which we are not worthy to ask,
except through the merits and mediation
of Jesus Christ our Savior;
who lives and reigns
with you and the Holy Spirit,
one God, for ever and ever. Amen.

(Collect for Proper 22, page 234, The Book of Common Prayer)

_____

_____

_____

_____

_____

_____

_____

_____

_____

_____

_____

_____

_____

_____

_____

_____

Most loving Father, whose will it is for us to give thanks for all things, to fear nothing but the loss of you, and to cast all our care on you who cares for us: Preserve us from faithless fears and worldly anxieties, that no clouds of this mortal life may hide from us the light of that love which is immortal, and which you have manifested to us in your Son Jesus Christ our Lord; who lives and reigns with you, in the unity of the Holy Spirit, one God, now and for ever. Amen.

(Collect for the Eighth Sunday after the Epiphany, page 216, The Book of Common Prayer)

PRAYING THE LORD'S PRAYER

Before we start diving into different prayer forms, let's start with the prayer Jesus gave us and take the time to really look at the words. Most of us can probably rattle off this prayer from rote memory. Even my young kids can run through this prayer, but I doubt they really understand the words they're saying. Are they even saying the right words? What about you?

This is a powerful prayer when you really take it to heart. Read Matthew 6:5-15 to see how Jesus taught his disciples to pray.

"And when you pray, do not be like the hypocrites, for they love to pray standing in the synagogues and on the street corners to be seen by others. Truly I tell you, they have received their reward in full. But when you pray, go into your room close the door and pray to your Father, who is unseen. Then your Father, who sees what is done in secret, will reward you. And when you pray, do not keep on babbling like pagans, for they think they will be heard because of their many words. Do not be like them, for your Father knows what you need before you ask him.

"This, then, is how you should pray:

"'Our Father in heaven,
hallowed be your name,
your kingdom come,
your will be done,
    on earth as it is in heaven.
Give us today our daily bread.
And forgive us our debts,
    as we also have forgiven our debtors.
And lead us not into temptation,
    but deliver us from the evil one.'

For if you forgive other people when they sin against you, your heavenly Father will also forgive you. But if you do not forgive others their sins, your Father will not forgive your sins."

How can I make the Lord's Prayer more meaningful?

1) Read it and focus on the words

Pray the Lord's Prayer, but instead of just reciting it from memory, take the time to read it. Pause over each phrase and take in what those words mean. What do those words mean to you right now, in your life today? What do you want them to mean? Make some notes in the margin below for each section of the Lord's Prayer.

Our Father, who art in heaven,
hallowed be thy Name,

thy kingdom come,
thy will be done,
on earth as it is in heaven.

Give us this day our daily bread.
And forgive us our trespasses,
as we forgive those
who trespass against us.

And lead us not into temptation,
but deliver us from evil.

For thine is the kingdom,
and the power, and the glory,
for ever and ever. Amen.

> "I used to think the Lord's Prayer was a short prayer; but as I live longer, and see more of life, I begin to believe there is no such thing as getting through it. If a man, in praying that prayer, were to be stopped by every word until he had thoroughly prayed it, it would take him a lifetime."
> –Henry Ward Beecher

2) Put it into your own words

Next, put this prayer into your own words. How would you express these same thoughts to God? Maybe write down your version and pray it again. Take the time to make this prayer even more personal and meaningful. Then, see how it impacts you the next time you pray it in church. Does it sink in a little deeper, feel more powerful, and become more than just words we recite?

The Lord's Prayer

Our Father, who art in heaven,
hallowed be thy Name,

thy kingdom come,
thy will be done,
on earth as it is in heaven.
Give us this day our daily bread.

And forgive us our trespasses,
as we forgive those
who trespass against us.

And lead us not into temptation,
but deliver us from evil.

For thine is the kingdom,
and the power, and the glory,
for ever and ever. Amen.

Example in My Own Words:

Heavenly Father, you are the greatest in all the world, may this world see more of you and follow your ways.

Help me remember your great provision, that you provide what I need.

Forgive me when I mess up and don't always do the things you want of me.

Help me avoid all the temptations of this world and instead follow your way.

You are indeed the greatest and I worship you with all my heart, my soul, and my mind. I want the world to see your glory shine through me. Amen.

GUIDE FOR PRAYING DEEP TODAY:

Today, write your own version of the Lord's Prayer. Start by praying the Lord's Prayer, paying attention to the words. Then, write your own version. Don't worry about keeping it to the same length. This is YOUR version, so expand anywhere your heart feels pulled. Try to include something for each phrase in the Lord's Prayer.

_____

_____

_____

_____

_____

_____

_____

_____

_____

_____

_____

_____

_____

_____

_____

_____

_____

_____

_____

_____
_____
_____
_____
_____
_____
_____
_____
_____
_____
_____
_____
_____
_____

Almighty God, whose blessed Son was led by the Spirit to be tempted by Satan: Come quickly to help us who are assaulted by many temptations; and, as you know the weaknesses of each of us, let each one find you mighty to save; through Jesus Christ your Son our Lord, who lives and reigns with you and the Holy Spirit, one God, now and for ever. Amen.

(Collect for the First Sunday of Lent page 218, The Book of Common Prayer)

A.C.T.S. Template for Prayer

I remember sitting through many college lectures on various theories and strategies and feeling so lost and overwhelmed. The descriptions were so lengthy and complex; the practical application so elusive. The professor would go on and on, elaborating the details and I'd just get lost. But then, inevitably, the professor would provide an illustration or a framework or an acronym that boiled it all down into something simple. Then, I got it - an "aha!"

As I read Matthew 6, Jesus' teaching on how to pray, I sometimes feel the same way. The language can be hard to follow and difficult to interpret just what this means for my every day prayer. The Lord's Prayer is beautiful, yet how do I learn from it to pray on my own?

Let me share an acronym to help break down the Lord's Prayer into its basic components so you can use Jesus' teaching to pray on your own.

A: Adoration

C: Confession

T: Thanksgiving

S: Supplication

A.C.T.S:Adoration.Confession.Thanksgiving.Supplication.

ADORATION

Tell God how wonderful He is. Worship Him and acknowledge His greatness.

"Our Father, who art in heaven, hallowed be thy name."

CONFESSION

Admit your sins, cry out your brokenness.

"forgive us our debts, as we also have forgiven our debtors"

THANKSGIVING

Say "thank you" to God for all He's done in your life.

"For thine is the kingdom and the power and the glory forever"

SUPPLICATION

Make your requests to God, asking Him for your own needs, as well as praying for others.

"Give us this day our daily bread…
Lead us not into temptation, but deliver us from evil"
"Your kingdom come, Your will be done, on earth as it is in heaven"

GUIDE FOR PRAYING DEEP TODAY:

Today, pray your version of an A.C.T.S prayer. Take time to have a good conversation with God over each section: Adoration, Confession, Thanksgiving, and Supplication.

_____

_____

_____

_____

_____

_____

_____

_____

_____

_____

_____

_____

_____

_____

_____

_____

_____

_____

_____

_____

_____

_____

_____

_____

_____

_____

_____

_____

_____

_____

_____

_____

_____

_____

Almighty God, you alone can bring into order the unruly wills and affections of sinners: Grant your people grace to love what you command and desire what you promise; that, among the swift and varied changes of the world, our hearts may surely there be fixed where true joys are to be found; through Jesus Christ our Lord, who lives and reigns with you and the Holy Spirit, one God, now and for ever. Amen.

(Collect for the Fifth Sunday of Lent page 219, The Book of Common Prayer)

PrayInG ScriPTure

Praying scriptures back to God is a powerful way to pray deep and build your prayer language. What better way to honor our majestic God than to use His own words to praise Him and pray to Him? It's also a way to dig deeper into scripture while you pray.

Choosing a scripture to pray:

- Open your Bible to any page and pray the passage that catches your eye.

- Keep a list of favorite verses and choose from that list. Maybe you have verses for specific needs.

- Pray from the week's lectionary readings. Look up the verses for the week at www.lectionarypage.net.

How to pray scripture:

READ the passage slowly, soak in the words, and take the verses to heart. You may even want to write it out on paper.

REFLECT on what the passage is saying to you. How does this passage apply to your life right now? How does it address your prayer needs? What words stand out to you and speak to your heart?

RESPOND to God by praying this passage back to him. Insert "I" or "me" in the passage to make it more personal. Or, insert a friend's name if you're praying the scripture for someone else. As you respond in prayer, consider these three responses:

- ***REJOICE*** in God's great goodness. Praise Him through the scripture.

- ***REPENT*** your mistakes and sins. How does this passage convict you?

- ***REQUEST*** prayer for your areas of need. Ask for God's promises and blessings from this passage.

RECEIVE God's response to your prayer by taking a moment of silence to listen. What is He putting on your heart in response to your prayer?

Praying scripture to deepen your prayer language:

As an example of praying scripture, let's look at Mark 8:31-38. Read through this passage, then read an example of my prayer below.

> Then Jesus began to teach his disciples that the Son of Man must undergo great suffering, and be rejected by the elders, the chief priests, and the scribes, and be killed, and after three days rise again. He said all this quite openly. And Peter took him aside and began to rebuke him. But turning and looking at his disciples, he rebuked Peter and said, "Get behind me, Satan! For you are setting your mind not on divine things but on human things."
>
> He called the crowd with his disciples, and said to them, "If any want to become my followers, let them deny themselves and take up their cross and follow me. For those who want to save their life will lose it, and those who lose their life for my sake, and for the sake of the gospel, will save it. For what will it profit them to gain the whole world and forfeit their life? Indeed, what can they give in return for their life? Those who are ashamed of me and of my words in this adulterous and sinful generation, of them the Son of Man will also be ashamed when he comes in the glory of his Father with the holy angels."

Heavenly Father,

You sent your son, your only son, the Son of Man, Jesus Christ, down to earth to teach us and save us. For our sake, he suffered great pain and rejection and was killed. Yet, in Your great majesty, he rose from the dead to live in Your glory with the holy angels, to give us new life in You.

God, how I want to follow you, to take up my cross and follow you, yet too often I'm like Peter. Too often, I'm focused on earthly matters, human priorities, my own wants.

Help me lift my eyes and set my mind on divine things instead of human things. Help me take up my cross and follow You. To lose my life for Your sake and the sake of the gospel. I don't want to be ashamed of You in this world, but instead be bold to proclaim Your goodness. For, in the end, what good will it do me to gain the whole world, yet forfeit my own life?   Amen.

GUIDE FOR PRAYING DEEP TODAY:

Today, use 1 Thessalonians 5:16-22 to practice these steps for praying scripture. Read the passage, reflect on its meaning to you, respond in prayer (write your prayer below), then listen and receive God's response.

1 Thessalonians 5:16-22:
Rejoice always, pray continually, give thanks in all circumstances; for this is God's will for you in Christ Jesus. Do not quench the Spirit. Do not treat prophecies with contempt but test them all; hold on to what is good, reject every kind of evil.

_____

_____

_____

_____

_____

_____

_____

_____

_____

_____

_____

_____

_____

_____

_____

_____

_____

_____

_____

_____

_____

_____

_____

_____

_____

_____

_____

_____

O God, whose Son Jesus is the good shepherd of your people: Grant that when we hear his voice we may know him who calls us each by name, and follow where he leads; who, with you and the Holy Spirit, lives and reigns, on God, for ever and ever. Amen.

(Collect for the Fourth Sunday of Easter, page 225, The Book of Common Prayer)

The 5 Finger prayer

According to some studies, 65% of us are visual learners, meaning we learn better from pictures, graphics, illustrations and charts. If you are in this group of visual learners, or even in the 5% of kinesthetic learners who need touch and movement, then you may like this prayer framework even better than the A.C.T.S template.

The 5 Finger Prayer

This prayer is said to have been created by Pope Francis, long before he was elected to be the Pope. It shows his sense of simplicity and can be a great prayer format to share with your children.

THUMB: The thumb is the closest finger to you. Start by praying for those who are closest to you. They are the easiest to remember. To pray for our dear ones is a "sweet obligation."

INDEX FINGER: The next finger is the index or pointer finger. Pray for those who teach you, instruct you, and heal you. They need the support and wisdom to show direction to others. Always keep them in your prayers.

MIDDLE FINGER: This finger is the tallest. It reminds us of our leaders, the governors, and those who have authority. They need God's guidance.

RING FINGER: The fourth finger is the ring finger. Even though it may surprise you, it is our weakest finger. It should remind you to pray for the weakest, the sick, or those plagued by problems. They need your prayers.

PINKIE: Finally, we have our pinkie, the smallest finger of all. Your pinkie should remind you to pray for yourself. When you are done praying for the other four groups, you will be able to see your own needs, but in the proper perspective.

Praying the 5 Finger Prayer

1) Pray for those most dear to you

2) Pray for those who teach and heal

3) Pray for leaders and those in authority

4) Pray for the weak, the sick, the suffering

5) Pray for your own needs

GUIDE FOR PRAYING DEEP TODAY:

Try out the 5 Finger Prayer today, taking your time to pray over each finger. Pray aloud or write out your prayer here. How did praying for yourself last feel? Did it change how you prayed?

_____

_____

_____

_____

_____

_____

_____

_____

_____

_____

_____

_____

_____

_____

_____

_____

_____

_____

_____

_____

_____

_____

_____

_____

_____

_____

_____

_____

_____

_____

_____

Oh God, the creator and preserver of all mankind, we humbly beseech thee for all sorts and conditions of men; that thou wouldest be pleased to make thy ways known unto them, thy saving health unto all nations. More especially we pray for thy holy Church universal; that it may be so guided and governed by thy good Spirit, that all who profess and call themselves Christians may be led into the way of truth, and hold the faith in unity of spirit, in the bond of peace, and in righteousness of life. Finally, we commend to thy fatherly goodness all those who are in any ways afflicted or distressed, in mind, body, or estate; [especially those for whom our prayers are desired]; that it may please thee to comfort and relieve them according to their several necessities, giving them patience under their sufferings, and a happy issue out of all their afflictions. And this we beg for Jesus Christ's sake. Amen.

(Collect for All Sorts and Conditions of Men, page 814, The Book of Common Prayer)

USING EVERY DAY PRAYER PROMPTS

The fire station just down the road from us has a helipad which hosts the local air ambulance crew. My kids love to look for the helicopter when we drive by. A particular highlight is if we happen to drive by as it's landing or taking off. The helicopter has become part of our daily lives as we see it flying overhead and run outside to see if it's heading out or coming home.

When the kids were just old enough to start learning about prayer, I suggested we pray for the helicopter anytime we saw it was away from its base. So, whenever we see the helicopter is out we say a quick prayer in the car together for the people the crew is going to help and safety for the crew. We've also added prayers anytime we see a fire truck or ambulance go by with lights flashing.

God, please go with the helicopter and keep the crew safe. Give them strength and power to help those in need. Be with the people the helicopter is going to help. Give them healing and wrap them in your love and support.

Use something you see daily as prompt for prayer.

These are everyday prompts for prayer we can use to connect with God in our daily lives. It's a quick reminder to say a prayer for someone. While it may not be a deep connection to say a quick prayer as we're driving, it has deepened my overall prayer life by putting prayer into my mind throughout the day. I found the more I used these prompts and began to pray these little prayers, the more I thought to pray throughout the day about other things going on in my life.

Prayer should be woven into our everyday thoughts, not only during a specific time.

God wants us to include Him in our thoughts and decisions, to allow Him to enter those conversations that roll around in our minds. For me, the car is where I have most of my internal conversations. Those discussions that seem to bounce around my head, the place where worry and debate are most intense. Being prompted for some basic prayers for our first responders also serves as a prompt to invite God into my internal conversation.

What if your prayer prompt was the thing which frustrates you most?

What do you feel when you are stopped at a red light? Frustrated, anxious, stressed? What about thankful or joyful? Probably not, but would you believe I've found a way to make red lights an enjoyable part of the day?

I decided to use red lights as an every day prayer prompt. Every time I'm stopped at one, I say a quick prayer of thanksgiving. I've gotten the kids involved, too, so we each call out something for which we're thankful.

Some days it's a challenge to think of something, especially after we've hit a number of red lights in a row. Yet, there's always something. It's helped us move beyond the standard blessings (family, God, teachers, etc.) and think more creatively. Like, thank you for red lights, so we can share our blessings.

Prayer changes our heart and our attitude.

I don't get so frustrated at red lights anymore. Now they're an opportunity to make a quick connection with God and thank Him for something from that moment. I love how my kids have embraced it and I enjoy hearing what they find to pray. It's cultivating a thankful heart in all of us and helps keep us in a more positive spirit throughout the day.

What do you see often throughout your day that can serve as a prayer prompt?

Getting Started

1. Choose something you see frequently throughout your daily routine.

2. Decide a quick prayer you'll say each time you see it. This doesn't have to be a set prayer, just give yourself some kind of guide. Maybe you'll pray for someone on your prayer list, pray for safety and healing, pray for thankfulness, pray for strength, pray for guidance, or pray for God to reveal Himself more fully in your life.

3. As you see your prompt throughout your day, just say a quick prayer in your mind, or aloud if you want to make it a family activity. Don't worry if you forget, just try again the next time. It make take some time to develop into a habit.

Examples of Every Day Prayer Prompts:

- See a fire truck or ambulance… pray for first responders and healing and strength for those they help.

- Stopped at a red light… tell God thank you for a blessing.

- Turn on a lamp or light a candle… ask God to reveal Himself more fully in your life.

- Hug your child… pray for God's protection over your child.

- See a bench… pray for the homeless and those who may have little more than a bench to sleep upon.

- Look at a favorite tree… pray for a friend to grow in his or her relationship with God, to grow deeper roots of faith.

- Eat a treat… pray for the hungry.

- Before you get out of your car at work… pray for your day.

Guide For Praying Deep Today:

Write out a list of prompts you might use for every day prayers. List as many as you can. Then, read over the list and circle one or two that tug at your heart the most. Write down how you'll incorporate these into your day. Then, pray about these, asking God to help you build these prayers into your every day routines.

_____

_____

_____

_____

_____

_____

_____

_____

_____

_____

_____

_____

_____

_____

_____

_____

_____

_____

_____

_____

_____

_____

_____

_____

_____

_____

_____

_____

_____

_____

_____

_____

_____

_____

_____

Almighty and eternal God, so draw our hearts to you, so guide our minds, so fill our imaginations, so control our wills, that we may be wholly yours, utterly dedicated to you, and then use us, we pray, as you will, and always to your glory and the welfare of your people; through our Lord and Savior Jesus Christ. Amen.

(A Prayer of Self-Dedications, page 832, The Book of Common Prayer)

prayer DOODLING

I almost can't resist coloring in outlined letters, especially if I'm on a conference call. The margins of my textbooks were always full of designs, headlines and other outlined shapes filled in. Doodling is practically compulsive for most of us.

I remember my mother's telephone notes were always full of doodles. As she noted down names, numbers, and other pertinent details, she'd fill the space around them with elaborate doodles.

Why do we do this? Isn't doodling just a waste of time, a bad habit we should have given up in school?

Doodling improves focus and generates new insight

According to the Wall Street Journal, Sunni Brown, author of "The Doodle Revolution," says doodling is a "thinking tool" that "affects how we process information and solve problems." She also claims every president from Washington to Nixon doodled, along with numerous great writers (Mark Twain, Sylvia Plath) and inventors (Thomas Edison).

How can doodling help us pray?

Sybil MacBeth wrote a book called "Praying in Color: Drawing a New Path to God (Active Prayer Series)" that outlines a way to pray through doodles. This might be my favorite new prayer method. I'm no artist and art projects tend to make me anxious, but I've found this method very relaxing and meaningful. It's a creative outlet and a way to stay focused in prayer.

Her website (www.prayingincolor.com) has some wonderful illustrations and explanations on prayer doodling, but I'll give you a brief overview here. You can pray different things through this method - names of God, names of people you're praying for, scripture verses, or other prayer needs. The key is to release the words to God as you draw. Make your doodling time prayerful.

Doodling Your Prayers:

Getting Started

1. Start with a blank piece of paper.

2. In the center, write a name for God, name of someone for whom you're praying, or a scripture verse.

3. Draw a shape around the words to start the doodle. This is your prayer space. Start to doodle around it, releasing your words to God in prayer. Doodle in silence or talk to God if you feel led.

4. Add other people, other names for God, or other parts of the scripture verse to your paper. Draw a shape around each set of new words to create a separate prayer space. Doodle around these and pray.

5. Pause and say "amen" between each prayer space you add.

Don't worry about the artistic quality of your doodles. Just let your pen draw and your mind focus on your prayers. In case you find the beautiful examples in Sybil's book intimidating, these are examples of my doodle prayers. If I can do these, then so can you.

Guide For Praying Deep Today:

For today's prayer, use these blank pages to try prayer doodling as you pray for others. Think about those on your prayer list, those closest to you, and those in need of prayer.

- As a name comes into your mind, write it down.

- Draw a shape around the name creating a prayer space.

- Doodle around the shape as you hold that person in mind and heart.

- Write out your prayers for that person or just pray as you draw and color.

- As you move onto the next name, close that prayer with an "amen" or "Lord, hear my prayer."

Journal about your experience doodling your prayers. Did you like this form of prayer? Did it bring you greater focus in your prayers? Why or why not?

_____
_____
_____
_____
_____
_____
_____
_____
_____
_____
_____
_____
_____
_____
_____
_____

Almighty God, we entrust all who are dear to us to your never-failing care and love, for this life and the life to come, knowing that you are doing for them better things than we can desire or pray for; through Jesus Christ our Lord. Amen.

(A Prayer for those we Love, page 831, The Book of Common Prayer)

Praying From Psalms

My least favorite part of high school English class was the poetry, and goodness was there a lot of poetry. Seems like every week we'd have to read another poem. I wanted to read through the poems as quickly as I read other books, but poems need you to linger and soak in the words to find your own meaning and relevance.

The Bible has its own book of poetry, Psalms. I hear people talk about how this is their favorite book in the Bible and how they are drawn to particular Psalms, but it's the book I always skip over. I'd rather get caught up in the narratives and teachings within other books. That is, until I began praying the Psalms…

Psalms are poetry, music, and prayer

Extemporaneous prayer - praying from your own heart, with your own words - is wonderful and a great way to have conversation with God. But, what if you're not sure what words to pray? What if you're not confident in how to get started? What if you want to experience something more from your prayers?

Praying God's words back to Him is a powerful way to pray

The book of Psalms is a great place to start praying scripture. Within the Psalms, every human emotion is covered, from grief, despair, and confession to praise, joy, and thanksgiving. Timeless laments and evergreen praises, words that have been sung and prayed for thousands of years. Ancient words that still speak to our lives today.

Using the Psalms as your prayer book

Choose a Psalm and read through it. Then, read it again, lingering over the words that speak to your heart. Soak in the emotions and the hope of God's promises.

As you connect with the words in the Psalm, begin to say those words to God in prayer. Pray for yourself and for others using the words of the Psalm.

Write out your own prayer from the verses that spoke the most to you.

Choosing a Psalm to Pray

You can choose your Psalm in different ways. Maybe you are familiar with the book and have a favorite one or one you know will speak to your situation that day. Or, simply open your Bible to the book of Psalms and pray the first one you see.

Another option is to pray from a daily or weekly list of selected Psalms. I've always wanted to just randomly open my Bible and have that experience of seeing just the right passage. I know that works, but it's hard for me to trust the random page turning. Instead, I've found using the lectionary to be a similar process, yet with some order.

Using the Lectionary to choose your Psalm

The Revised Common Lectionary is a three-year cycle of weekly scripture selections used by a majority of Protestant churches in the US and Canada and also closely follows the lectionary used by the Roman Catholic Church. It generally includes a reading from the Old Testament, a Psalm, a reading from one of the Gospels and a reading from the Epistles. The readings are built around the seasons of the Church Year, which reflects the life of Jesus.

One of the things I love about using the Lectionary to select Psalms and scripture for my prayers is that I'm more connected to the scripture used in my church service on Sunday. I have prayed or studied the scripture I'll hear read or preached on Sunday. It's my way to go deeper in the message that week.

You can find the listing of weekly lectionary readings at this website: www.lectionarypage.net.

There are also calendars for praying Psalms (like the one below), outlining particular Psalms you can pray each day of the month. These take you through all the Psalms in 30 days, so it can seem a bit overwhelming, but just choose one of the selections for the day you're praying.

Day	Morning	Evening	Day	Morning	Evening	Day	Morning	Evening
1	1-5	6-8	11	56-58	59-61	21	105	106
2	9-11	12-13	12	62-64	65-67	22	107	108-109
3	14-17	18	13	68	69-70	23	110-113	114-115
4	19-21	22-23	14	71-72	73-74	24	116-118	119:1-32
5	24-26	27-29	15	75-77	78	25	119:33-72	119:73-104
6	30-31	32-34	16	79-81	82-85	26	119:105-144	119:145-176
7	35-36	37	17	86-88	89	27	120-125	126-131
8	38-40	41-43	18	90-92	93-94	28	132-135	136-138
9	44-46	47-49	19	95-97	98-101	29	139-140	141-143
10	50-52	53-55	20	102-103	104	30	144-146	147-150

GUIDE FOR PRAYING DEEP TODAY:

Read Psalm 86 and use its words as your prayer today.
Write out your own version of a prayer from Psalm 86 here.

Psalm 86:

1 Hear me, Lord, and answer me,
   for I am poor and needy.

2 Guard my life, for I am faithful
   to you;
   save your servant who trusts in you.
   You are my God;

3 have mercy on me, Lord,
   for I call to you all day long.

4 Bring joy to your servant, Lord,
   for I put my trust in you.

5 You, Lord, are forgiving and good,
   abounding in love to all who
   call to you.

6 Hear my prayer, Lord;
   listen to my cry for mercy.

7 When I am in distress, I call to you,
   because you answer me.

8 Among the gods there is none
   like you, Lord;
   no deeds can compare with yours.

9 All the nations you have made
   will come and worship before
   you, Lord;
   they will bring glory to your name.

10 For you are great and do
   marvelous deeds;
   you alone are God.

11 Teach me your way, Lord,
   that I may rely on your faithfulness;
   give me an undivided heart,
   that I may fear your name.

12 I will praise you, Lord my God,
   with all my heart;
   I will glorify your name forever.

13 For great is your love toward me;
   you have delivered me from
   the depths,
   from the realm of the dead.

14 Arrogant foes are attacking me,
   O God; ruthless people are
   trying to kill me—
   they have no regard for you.

15 But you, Lord, are a
   compassionate and gracious God,
   slow to anger, abounding in love
   and faithfulness.

16 Turn to me and have mercy on me;
   show your strength in behalf of
   your servant;
   save me, because I serve you
   just as my mother did.

17 Give me a sign of your goodness,
   that my enemies may see it and
   be put to shame,
   for you, Lord, have helped me and
   comforted me.

_____

_____

_____

_____

_____

_____

_____

_____

_____

_____

_____

_____

_____

Almighty God, who has promised to hear the petitions of those who ask in your Son's Name: We beseech you mercifully to incline your ear to us who have now made our prayers and supplications to you; and grant that those things which we have faithfully asked according to your will, may effectually be obtained, to the relief of our necessity; and to the setting forth of your glory; through Jesus Christ our Lord. Amen.

(For the Answering of Prayer, page 834, The Book of Common Prayer)

GOSPEL CONTEMPLATION

Hiding my phone's light under the covers so I wouldn't wake my husband, I stayed up late to finish the last pages of the book. I knew how it would end, but I was so wrapped up in this familiar, yet enthrallingly new, story that I couldn't put the book down.

I was reading "The Fisherman," a novel based on the Gospel from Peter's perspective. I'd been studying Peter for some months and knew the stories inside out. Yet, in this novelized version, with flowing dialog and filled-in scenes, I found myself in the story. By the time Peter met Jesus after the resurrection, I was in tears.

How had this book moved me to tears? Over a story I knew by heart? This book had drawn me into the story in a way scripture alone hadn't. It made the story and the characters more real, the emotions and events more palpable.

Engaging scripture through prayer and imagination

The prayer technique of Ignatian Gospel Contemplation is way to similarly engage more deeply in scripture. In this form of prayer, you place yourself in the scene of a Gospel story and engage deeply in the sights, sounds, smells, emotions, and energy of the story. Like the novel I read of Peter's role in the Gospel story, use your imagination to bring the scenes of Jesus' story to life for you.

This form of prayer was developed by Saint Ignatius Loyola, founder of the Jesuits, as a way to more closely connect with Jesus and the story of his life and ministry. Sometimes we so quickly skim over the written word, but when we take the time to listen to the story and place ourselves in it, the words can become so much more powerful.

Enter the story through Ignatian Gospel Contemplation:

1. Choose a passage from the Gospel where Jesus is interacting with others.

2. Ask God to be present and speak to you through His word.

3. Read through the selected passage at least two times, until the story becomes familiar.

4. Close your eyes and imagine the scene. Focus in on Jesus. What is he doing? What is he saying? How is he interacting with others? Focus on the others in the scene. What are they saying? What emotions are they feeling?

5. Engage the scene with all your senses. What do you see, smell, hear, touch, and taste? How is the crowd moving? How are people reacting to Jesus? How are YOU responding to Jesus?

6. Close with prayer. Spend some time speaking your heart to Jesus about what you experienced through the story.

GUIDE FOR PRAYING DEEP TODAY:

Read Matthew 14:22-33. Place yourself in the scene, in the boat with the disciples. Can you smell the sea, feel the wind and rain of the storm, taste the water as it hits your lips, feel the boat tossing in the waves, sense the fear and worry of all on the boat? Take note how you feel as the scene progresses. How are the others reacting to Jesus? How are you responding to Jesus? Journal your experience.

Matthew 14:22-33: Jesus Walks on the Water

22 Immediately Jesus made the disciples get into the boat and go on ahead of him to the other side, while he dismissed the crowd. 23 After he had dismissed them, he went up on a mountainside by himself to pray. Later that night, he was there alone, 24 and the boat was already a considerable distance from land, buffeted by the waves because the wind was against it.

25 Shortly before dawn Jesus went out to them, walking on the lake. 26 When the disciples saw him walking on the lake, they were terrified. "It's a ghost," they said, and cried out in fear.

27 But Jesus immediately said to them: "Take courage! It is I. Don't be afraid."

28 "Lord, if it's you," Peter replied, "tell me to come to you on the water."

29 "Come," he said.

Then Peter got down out of the boat, walked on the water and came toward Jesus. 30 But when he saw the wind, he was afraid and, beginning to sink, cried out, "Lord, save me!"

31 Immediately Jesus reached out his hand and caught him. "You of little faith," he said, "why did you doubt?"

32 And when they climbed into the boat, the wind died down. 33 Then those who were in the boat worshiped him, saying, "Truly you are the Son of God."

Grant us, Lord, not to be anxious about earthly things, but to love things heavenly; and even now, while we are placed among things that are passing away, to hold fast to those that shall endure; through Jesus Christ our Lord, who lives and reigns with you and the Holy Spirit, one God, for ever and ever. Amen.

(Collect for the Proper 20, page 234, The Book of Common Prayer)

PRAYING a SONG

I was reading from the Psalms when I had a revelation. "I've heard these words before! They're in that song I've been singing with on the radio." Don't ask my why it took so long to realize that most Christian music has foundations in scripture and often uses lines directly from scripture in the lyrics.

Once I began to notice, though, music began to bring scripture to life in new ways. I started to connect both the traditional hymns we sing in church and the contemporary Christian music I hear on the radio to the scripture on which they're based.

Just as we've talked about praying from scripture, so can we pray from songs. The Psalms were originally songs, yet now we only have the lyrics so we read and pray them. Songs connect with our emotions and hearts. The language of the lyrics is rhythmic and poetic. It works its way into our hearts and souls, so why not use music in our prayers?

Singing our prayers to God

In my childhood church, we always sang "amen" at the end of every hymn. I didn't think much about it then, but that word signified the prayerfulness of the song. We were indeed praying as we sang. Although most churches have phased out the "amen," songs are still a form of prayer.

We see numerous examples in the Bible of song as prayer. The book of Psalms were originally songs, though now we most often use them as prayer. In Acts, we see Paul and Silas praying and singing as they were locked in the prison.

Using Music as Prayer

Who doesn't like to hear something nice? We all love when a friend says something nice - compliments our hair or shoes, praises something we've done. God's no different. He loves to hear us praise Him.

So, what are some ways we can use music as prayer?

1. Sing along to your favorite Christian song (contemporary or traditional) and think about the words as you sing. Sing the words as if praying to God.

2. Find the lyrics to the song and read them as a prayer. Sometimes reading song lyrics makes them feel new and more purposeful.

If you've ever wondered what scripture a particular song is using - or want to find songs using a specific verse - check out this website: Word to Worship (http://wordtoworship.com/)

> *I wish to see all art, principally music, in the service of Him who gave and created them. Music is a fair and glorious gift of God. I would not for the world forego my humble share of music. Singers are never sorrowful, but are merry, and smile through their troubles in song. Music makes people kinder, gentler, more staid and reasonable. I am strongly persuaded that after theology there is no art that can be placed on a level with music; for besides theology, music is the only art capable of affording peace and joy of the heart...the devil flees before the sound of music almost as much as before the Word of God. ~ Martin Luther*

Guide For Praying Deep Today:

Pray "Amazing Grace" by reading the words aloud. Try to keep your-self from singing. Instead focus on the words and what they mean to you. Write a prayer from the words and verses that speak most to your heart. How does this song lead you to pray?

Amazing Grace

Amazing grace! How sweet the sound!
That saved a wretch like me!
I once was lost, but now am found;
Was blind, but now I see.

'Twas grace that taught my heart to fear,
And grace my fears relieved.
How precious did that grace appear
The hour I first believed!

Thru many dangers, toils and snares
I have already come;
'Tis grace hath brought me safe thus far,
And grace will lead me home.

The Lord has promised good to me,
His Word my hope secures;
He will my Shield and Portion be,
As long as life endures.

When we've been there ten thousand years,
Bright shining as the sun,
We've no less days to sing God's praise
Than when we'd first begun.

_____

_____

_____

_____

_____

_____

Accept, O Lord, our thanks and praise for all that you have done for us. We thank you for the splendor of the whole creation, for the beauty of this world, for the wonder of life, and for the mystery of love.

We thank you for the blessing of family and friends, and for the loving care which surrounds us on every side.

We thank you for setting us at tasks which demand our best efforts, and for leading us to accomplishments which satisfy and delight us.

We thank you also for those disappointments and failures that lead us to acknowledge our dependence on you alone.

Above all, we thank you for your Son Jesus Christ; for the truth of his Word and the example of his life; for his steadfast obedience, by which he overcame temptation; for his dying, through which he overcame death; and for his rising to life again, in which we are raised to the life of your kingdom.

Grant us the gift of your Spirit, that we may know him and make him known; and through him, at all times and in all places, may give thanks to you in all things. Amen.

(A General Thanksgiving Prayer, page 836, The Book of Common Prayer)

Praying Deep: Day 13
Listening Through Lectio Divina

Have you ever had a Bible verse jump off the page at you? As you're reading, a phrase or words just seem to speak to your heart unlike any others on the page? I was taken aback the first time this happened, couldn't understand how these words seemed to speak so profoundly and personally to me. Now, it's one of my favorite phenomena of studying God's word. How the Bible is a living text and God can speak through its words to the core of our hearts.

Listening for God's words through scripture

Lectio Divina is another way to connect with God's word. It's sometimes described as reading scripture with the "ear of the heart," as if in a conversation with God.

Lectio Divina is translated as "divine reading" and is an ancient spiritual practice, dating back to the 6th century and still practiced worldwide today. It is a process of reading, reflecting, responding, and resting in a piece of scripture. It's a way to engage God in a conversation and listen for His words to you.

Allow the "ear of your heart" to listen for God's still small voice

This has become one of my favorite forms of prayer. I love the intimacy of choosing a small verse of scripture and diving deep into it. Soaking in each word and then listening for what God wants me to hear. Sometimes He speaks something related to the scripture and sometimes the scripture is a spark for something else He wants me to hear.

How to pray using Lectio Divina

Choose a passage of scripture. You'll want to select something short, maybe just a verse or two.

1. **READ** the verse slowly, several times, listening with the "ear of the heart." Is there a word or phrase that begins to stand out to you? Begin to repeat that word or phrase over and over slowly, soaking your heart in the words.

2. **REFLECT** on the words, attentive to what speaks to your heart. Sit in the silence and allow God the space to speak to you as you turn the words over in your mind.

3. **RESPOND** to what you heard from God and how the words spoke to your heart. Offer up a prayer of praise, thanksgiving, or petition, depending on how you're moved. Continue turning your word or phrase over and over in your mind.

4. **REST** in God. Sit in the silence and just "be" with God for a few minutes. Open your heart to God's presence and allow His words to permeate your soul.

You may want to journal your experience so you can see how God is moving in your life. Record the verse you used and what you heard God speak to your heart.

Guide for Praying Deep Today:

Using Matthew 11:28-30, try to use the steps outlined here to experience Lectio Divina. Read the passage several times, slowly. Reflect on the words, settling your focus on the words or phrase that catches your heart. Respond to what you hear from God. Rest in silence with God and open your heart to His words. Spend at least 15-20 minutes on this exercise. At the end, journal your experience. What word(s) or phrase stood out to you? How did you hear God speak to your heart? How did it feel to sit in silence with God? How will you respond to God's words?

Matthew 11:28-30:

"Come to me, all you who are weary and burdened, and I will give you rest.

Take my yoke upon you and learn from me, for I am gentle and humble in heart, and you will find rest for your souls.

For my yoke is easy and my burden is light."

_____

_____

_____

_____

_____

_____

_____

_____

_____

_____

_____

_____

Blessed Lord, who caused all holy Scriptures to be written for our learning: Grant us so to hear them, read, mark, learn, and inwardly digest them, that we may embrace and ever hold fast the blessed hope of everlasting life, which you have given us in our Savior Jesus Christ; who lives and reigns with you and the Holy Spirit, one God, for ever and ever. Amen.

(Collect for Proper 28, page 236, The Book of Common Prayer)

PrayinG THrouGH ManDaLas

When was the last time you colored with crayons? Until recently, when my daughter was old enough to begin coloring, I hadn't colored in decades. She wanted me to color with her, show her how to do it, and share time with her doing this new favorite activity. Only, I'm not artistic. At. All.

I get all closed up and anxious when I'm staring at a blank sheet of paper. I see pictures of friends doing those painting parties and think that'd be a fun girl's night out, but then I see the blank canvasses they started with and wonder how I'd ever produce something presentable.

I finally found a compromise that let me do coloring with my daughter without too much anxiety. In fact, I found it quite fun and relaxing. A coloring book! I found I could color within the lines and let my mind fall into the rhythm of coloring.

Creating art can be a form of prayer

One of the most ancient forms of prayer is the mandala and it's used across many different religions. The word mandala means "container of sacred essence" in Sanskrit. It originated as a spiritual practice in the 6th century BC out of the Hindu and Buddhist religions, but is now used by many others, including Christians.

Some of the more familiar forms of mandalas are the elaborate powdered marble designs made by Tibetan monks, the sand paintings made by the Navajo Indians, the Celtic knot, and the rose windows featured in many churches.

Active prayer to quiet the mind

You can use a mandala in your prayers in different ways. One is to find a template with a design (a coloring page) and color it in. Or you might draw your own design and color it in. You may even choose to create your own unique drawing, allowing your hand to create what comes to you in prayer.

With a mandala, you start with a circle. Create your prayer space. You don't have to stay within the lines, but this is your sacred space for prayer. You can draw your own circle on a blank piece of paper or print out a coloring page.

Then, begin to color. As you color, let your mind wander. This is not about the end result, but about the process of prayer. Spend time in prayer and talking with God as you color. Or, simply release yourself into His hands and allow God space to speak to your heart.

You can repeat scripture or a short prayer as you color, allow your mind to wander through the thoughts God places on your heart, or simply relax into the exercise.

Letting go of self to draw nearer to God

As I prayed through a mandala drawing this morning, I realized this one is a difficult prayer technique for me because I crave order and a plan. Starting with a blank sheet of paper and allowing myself to draw without a plan and an end result in mind is a challenge. I want to know that I'm working toward a great outcome.

Yet, I was reminded this exercise of prayer - really the whole faith journey - is about releasing myself to the process of following God's lead. He calls us to surrender, to release ourselves to His control, to focus on our journey, not our destination. I needed to let my mind wander and release my thoughts, so God could speak. I needed to accept that my picture may be meaningless and amateur by others' standards. I needed to release that this prayer is not about the drawing, but about the process of spending time with God.

Guide For Praying Deep Today:

Color a mandala for your prayer time today. Get lost in the coloring and clear your mind. Don't worry about the result, just focus on the process. I've provided two options - a mandala with pre-filled pattern you can color or a blank circle for you to create your own design.

Coloring a Mandala:

- Begin with a circle.

- Fill in the circle with your own patterns and art, or find a circle with a pattern already drawn and color it in.

- As you color or draw, spend time in prayer.

- Don't worry about what you are creating. This is about the process of praying, not the end result.

- Relax into the exercise. Allow your mind to wander through the thoughts God places on your heart.

- When have completed your mandala, spend some time to journal your experience, what you heard in your prayer time, or the insights you have from your completed mandala.

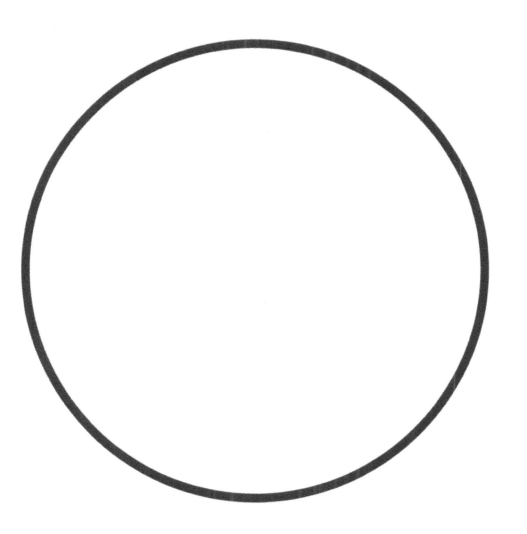

_____

_____

_____

_____

_____

_____

_____

_____

_____

_____

_____

_____

_____

_____

_____

*Heavenly Father, in you we live and move and have our
being: We humbly pray you so to guide and govern us by
your Holy Spirit, that in all the cares and occupations of our
life we may not forget you, but may remember that we are
ever walking in your sight; through Jesus Christ our Lord.
Amen.*

(A Collect for Guidance, page 100, The Book of Common Prayer)

LISTENING PRAYER

When my youngest was a baby, I cherished that last feeding of the night. I'd settle into the rocker in his room and, while he nursed, I'd sit in the dark hush of his room. As he fell asleep, I'd let the rhythmic rocking and gentle sound of his breathing calm my soul. I'd clear my head of thoughts and just listen, opening myself to God's presence.

Maybe it was easier then because I was so sleep-deprived and my inner monologue was exhausted too, but I could sit for 15-20 minutes of total silence and just be. Some nights, I didn't feel God's presence. Other nights I knew He was there, comforting this weary momma's soul. On a few special nights, I heard Him speak to my heart.

Silencing your thoughts to hear God's words

The thing is, we usually can't hear His still small voice unless we're quiet. So, in the dark quiet of a baby's room, rocking a sleeping little one, I was able to take that time to get quiet enough and truly just listen. I had no where else to be in that moment, no other task more important than getting the baby to sleep, so I could focus on listening for God.

As my son grew too big to rock to sleep, I worried that I'd lost my special time with God. How would I get that time and place to just be with Him in the silence?

Each season brings its own time and place to find stillness with God

I found that our prayer methods and forms of quiet time change with our life's seasons. In this season of life, I've found my best time with God is taking a long bath at night, after the kids are put to bed. I can sit in the candlelight, usually with soft music and allow the gentle hum of the jetted tub to clear my mind of the day's thoughts. I can sit with God and listen and pray. Or, I'll get up very early in the morning, before the rest of the family wakes and sit with God in the hush of a still-sleeping house.

So, how do you find that quiet time with God? What is your special place? What is your technique to clear your mind and listen for His still small voice?

Prayer isn't always about words, sometimes it's just about listening

Sometimes we need to spend our prayer time just listening, allowing God the space to speak to our hearts. We used this listening prayer at a conference recently and it was one of the most moving parts of the day. We spent 3 minutes in silence with God, yet even in that short time I could see people visibly moved by how God was speaking to their hearts.

How to Pray a Listening Prayer

- Set aside some quiet time when you can focus.

- Take some deep breaths to clear your thoughts or use a breathing exercise.

- Close your eyes and clear your thoughts.

- Ask God to be with you in the silence and speak to your heart.

- Sit in the silence and listen for God. Start with 3 minutes and work up to 15 minutes or more.

- After your time of silence, reflect on the experience and how you felt God speaking to you. Take notes of what God places on your heart. Maybe use one color for God's words and another color for your thoughts and responses.

> *God speaks in the silence of the heart.*
> *Listening is the beginning of prayer.*
> *~Mother Teresa*

Guide For Praying Deep Today:

Spend 5 minutes in listening prayer today. This may feel like a long time, but try to give in to the silence. Set a timer, so you're not tempted to keep checking the time. Follow the steps on the previous page for listening prayer. Settle into the silence and listen for God speaking to heart.

After your 5 minutes (or longer), journal your experience. How was the experience of silence? What thoughts did God place on your heart? Do you feel any difference after the silence?

"Here's what I want you to do: Find a quiet, secluded place so you won't be tempted to role-play before God. Just be there as simply and honestly as you can manage. The focus will shift from you to God, and you will begin to sense his grace."

Matthew 6:6 (The Message)

_____

_____

_____

_____

_____

_____

_____

_____

_____

_____

_____

_____

_____

_____

_____

_____

Almighty God, the fountain of all wisdom, you know our necessities before we ask and our ignorance in asking: Have compassion on our weakness, and mercifully give us those things which for our unworthiness we dare not, and for our blindness we cannot ask; through the worthiness of your Son Jesus Christ our Lord, who lives and reigns with you and the Holy Spirit, one God, now and for ever. Amen.

(Collect for the Proper 11, page 231, The Book of Common Prayer)

WALKING THE LABYRINTH

For my 40th birthday, I asked my husband for a mini-retreat. I wanted to spend a couple of days alone in silent retreat - reading, writing, and spending time with God - and then a couple of days visiting my dearest friends from childhood. I needed a few days of soul renewal, to recharge as I entered this next year.

When I checked into the retreat center, I noticed they had a labyrinth on site. I'd always been curious about the practice of walking a labyrinth, so I decided to try it while I was there. The next day, I walked to the edge of the retreat center property, crossing the river that runs through, and finally found the labyrinth, nestled in the woods on the hillside.

I read over a flyer that explained the labyrinth and different ways to experience it, then stepped in and began to walk. I have to say this was a highlight of my retreat, a powerful and moving experience. I spent close to an hour there talking to God, listening for His voice, and hearing His direction for my life as I walked.

> *Although the Lord gives you the bread of adversity and the water of affliction, your teachers will be hidden no more; with your own eyes you will see them. Whether you turn to the right or to the left, your ears will hear a voice behind you, saying, "This is the way; walk in it."*
> *Isaiah 30:20-21*

Prayer through movement and pilgrimage

Saint Augustine once said, "Solvitur amvulando... It is solved by walking." Pilgrimage is a journey of spiritual significance and I think this can describe your walk through a labyrinth. It's a tool to help you walk in place as you make a spiritual journey with God.

A labyrinth is an ancient spiritual tool for prayer and meditation. In the middle ages, Christian pilgrims would travel to a cathedral to walk the labyrinth when they were unable to make a pilgrimage to Jerusalem during the Crusades.

It is not a maze, but a single path that leads to the center and back. It will twist and turn, but you will not get lost. Walking the labyrinth can be experienced as a metaphor for your own spiritual journey with all its twists, turns, and meandering. The point is not to figure out how to get to the center, but how to take the next step with God. Focus on the journey, not the destination.

Finding a Labyrinth

Labyrinths can be physically walked or you can do a virtual walk with a table-top version or even an online version. To find a labyrinth near you, search the labyrinth locator (www.labyrinthlocator.com).

If you don't live near a labyrinth or physically waking one is not an option, you can print out a table-top version and "walk" it with your finger (www.labyrinthsociety.org). I've been using one of these in my morning prayers and it's been an effective method of prayer for me, for when I can't physically walk a labyrinth.

Walking a Labyrinth

There is no single right way to experience a labyrinth. You only need to enter and follow the path. The labyrinth is a spiritual tool for prayer; a metaphor for your own spiritual journey and taking the next step with God. Walk to the center, pause there and spend time with God, then follow the path back out.

There are a few different approaches you may want to consider:

The "Inner Way"

- As you walk in, toward the center, pray for release of your fears, distractions, and resistances. *"Let go and let God."*

- At the center, pray for illumination, for the Holy Spirit to fill you. *"Breathe on me breath of God; fill me with life anew."*

- On the way out, pray for integration of the Spirit's guidance into your life. *"Thy will be done."*

Ask a Question

Maybe you have a question on your heart, a need that's troubling you, or are seeking God's direction on something in your life. Approach the labyrinth with that prayer. Spend your walk praying and talking with God about your particular question or need. Make sure, though, you allow ample silence in your walk to listen for the still small voice of God.

Gracious Attention

A third way to experience a labyrinth is called "Gracious Attention." In this method, simply quiet your mind and walk. Let go of all thoughts and just listen for God's voice as you walk. Maybe meditate or repeat a simple prayer or verse, such as "Come, Holy Spirit, come."

Guide For Praying Deep Today:

Today you are going to walk the labyrinth. I use a printed version like the one on the next page to virtually walk the labyrinth during my morning prayers. I have one printed on 11x17 paper, so it's easier to trace. On this smaller version, you may want to use a pencil or crayon to mark your path. Maybe use one color on the way in and another on the way out.

Take a few minutes before you begin to decide how you want to approach the labyrinth. Do you have a specific question or concern you want to discuss with God or do you simply want to walk and listen for His voice? Spend a few minutes in prayer to first prepare your heart for the experience.

Next, walk the labyrinth on the next page. Take your time. It's tempting to go quickly on a small printed labyrinth, but don't run through this. Take the time to listen for God's voice.

After you complete the labyrinth, journal about your experience and what you heard as you walked.

_____

_____

_____

_____

_____

_____

_____

_____

_____

_____

_____

_____

_____

_____

_____

_____

_____

Almighty and merciful God, it is only by your gift that your faithful people offer you true and laudable service: Grant that we may run without stumbling to obtain your heavenly promises; through Jesus Christ our Lord, who lives and reigns with you and the Holy Spirit, one God, now and for ever. Amen.

(Collect for Proper 26, page 235, The Book of Common Prayer)

PRAYING THE EXAMEN

The project was delivered, celebration lunch eaten, and we were all ready to move on to new things. Yet, one final meeting remained on the calendar. A meeting no one really wanted to have, yet one we knew was important (and mandatory). The "lessons learned" meeting. The essential debrief at the end of every project to review what went well and, more importantly, what could be done better next time.

The reviews are intended to be a transparent and honest evaluation of how a project went. We start by celebrating and documenting the things we did really well. You need to acknowledge the good and make sure you repeat those successes. Then, we dig into the harder work of reviewing what didn't go so well and why. To do this part well, you have to leave your ego at the door and be ready to look at yourself first. What could I have done better? It's much easier to call out all the other things that went wrong, but much more difficult to identify where YOU could have made a better impact.

A daily "debrief" with Jesus

Just as we do this review as part of our project management, the Examen prayer is a way to do this for your daily life. The Examen prayer is a like a performance review you hold with Jesus at the end of each day. To review what you did well that day and where you need improvement.

> *"We must lay before him what is in us; not what ought to be in us."*
> *~C.S. Lewis*

Celebrate the victories, learn from your mistakes and do better next time

If we want to grow closer to God's vision for our lives, we have to continually evaluate how we're doing and make necessary course corrections. We need to identify where we're doing well and keep doing those things. However, we also need to see where we still need improvement. It's important to identify our mistakes and learn from them so we can do better next time.

Doing a playback of your day with Jesus by your side is a great way to see your day's performance though his eyes. Ask Jesus to show you what you did well and where you need work. As you walk back through your day, you'll see certain things highlighted as good examples and others you'll see as areas for improvement, some of which may surprise you. What better way to stay motivated and moving forward in your walk of faith than a daily checkpoint with Jesus?

To pray the Examen:

Set aside some time at the end of the day (or even throughout the day) to reflect on the events of that day.

- Become aware of God's presence.

- Thank God for the day's gifts.

- Ask Holy Spirit for guidance.

- Playback the events, conversations and emotions of your day, looking for 2 positive and 2 negative aspects. Imagine you are reviewing your day with Jesus and talk about your actions and emotions throughout the day.

- Reconcile and resolve. Give thanks, apologize, ask for guidance - and then resolve to move forward and try better tomorrow.

GUIDE FOR PRAYING DEEP TODAY:

Today, pray the Examen. Review your past day using this prayer method. Play back each interaction as if you're watching a movie of your day. Imagine Jesus sitting by your side, providing guidance and analysis.

Journal your experience. Write out your two positives and two negatives. What did you learn from this experience?

_____

_____

_____

_____

_____

_____

_____

_____

_____

_____

_____

_____

_____

_____

_____

_____

_____

_____

_____

_____

_____

_____

_____

_____

_____

_____

_____

_____

_____

_____

_____

_____

_____

_____

_____

_____

Almighty God, you know that we have no power in ourselves to help ourselves: Keep us both outwardly in our bodies and inwardly in our souls, that we may be defended from all adversities which may happen to the body, and from all evil thoughts which may assault and hurt the soul; through Jesus Christ our Lord, who lives and reigns with you and the Holy Spirit, one God, for ever and ever. Amen.

(A Collect for the Third Sunday in Lent, page 218, The Book of Common Prayer)

LeanING INTO PRayer

My dad called as I was getting in the car to drive home from work. We hadn't talked in a few days, so we jumped right into the conversation. We talked about the things he'd been doing all week and the people he'd seen. Then it was my turn. As I continued to talk about my week, I suddenly became aware of his silence. "Dad, are you there?" Turns out the line had dropped some minutes back and I'd been talking to myself.

Prayer can often feel this way, can't it? Like we're talking to an empty line, a phone that's hung up on us and we're talking to no one. Have you ever found yourself asking: "Is God really listening to my prayers? Does He really care about little ol' me?"

The great news about God is His connection to us is way better than any telephone line. His connection is always on, always connected, and always listening.

God is always available, ready to listen to us.

We can go to God in prayer at any time of the day or night and He'll be there. He's always waiting for us to approach Him in prayer. When we seek Him, we'll find Him. That's His promise to us.

Then you will call on me and come and pray to me, and I will listen to you. You will seek me and find me when you seek me with all your heart.
- Jeremiah 29:12-13

119

God cares deeply about you.

When I think about my place in this great cosmic universe, I'm reminded I'm but a speck of dust, a grain of sand. Our lives are but a blink of an eye in God's timeline. So, does God really care about my life? Does He really know me personally?

I've struggled with these questions much of my life. Does the God of the universe, the great creator, the Almighty, really care about my little life and my little prayer concerns? Then, I began to dig deeper into scripture and found such profound promises from God how He loves and cares for each and every one of us.

For you created my inmost being;
you knit me together in my mother's womb.
- Psalm 139:13

He knew us before we were even born. In fact, He "knitted us in the womb." He knows us so intimately that He can number the hairs on our heads. I can't even do that for my own head, much less anyone else.

"And even the very hairs of your head are all numbered.
So don't be afraid; you are worth more than many sparrows."
- Matthew 10:30-31

Even when God seems silent, He's still listening. He just may be waiting to respond.

What about when God seems silent? When I don't feel His presence or hear His response? Is He still listening or has He abandoned me?

We have to remember that God's ways are bigger than ours. His timeline and vision are beyond our imagination. So, what seems like a long time to answer a prayer to us, may be only a second in God's time.

We also need to remember that God answers prayers in His ways, not always the way we want Him to. He promises us that when we approach Him with a sincere heart, He will always listen.

God even knows our prayers before we say the words. When God feels distant or silent, lean in and keep praying. Keep coming before Him with your prayers and open heart. Trust that He is listening and will answer your prayers.

Rejoice always, pray continually,
give thanks in all circumstances;
for this is God's will for you in Christ Jesus.
- 1 Thessalonians 5:28

Guide For Praying Deep Today:

On those days when God seems silent or isn't answering your prayers, try using a different prayer technique to connect to Him in another way. You may find it rejuvenates your prayer life and gives you a new perspective. Maybe you'll even hear from God in a fresh way.

Today, take the verse below and doodle it. Write it out - maybe in your own words or a shortened version. Draw doodles around the words, allowing your mind to absorb the words and focus on listening for God's voice.

*"Then you will call on me and
come and pray to me,
and I will listen to you.
You will seek me and find me
when you seek me with all your heart."*

Jeremiah 29:12-13

_____

_____

_____

_____

_____

_____

_____

_____

_____

_____

_____

_____

O God, by whom the meek are guided in judgment, and light riseth up in darkness for the godly: Grant us, in all our doubts and uncertainties, the grace to ask what you would have us to do, that the Spirit of wisdom may save us from all false choices, and that in your light we may see light, and in your straight path may not stumble; through Jesus Christ our Lord. Amen.

(A Prayer for Guidance, page 832, The Book of Common Prayer)

Pray Until You Pray

I was going through a tough time, overwhelmed with the issues I was facing in my life, and not living up to expectations I'd set for myself. The stress and worry were taking a toll and I needed something to change.

At the time, I believed in God, but didn't have Him as a focal point in my life. I had, though, recently started attending church again after a many year absence. The preacher invited me to meet him for coffee since I was a new visitor. As he listened to some of what was going on in my life, he began to counsel me to give these burdens over to God to carry.

Is prayer your steering wheel or your spare tire?
~ Corrie Ten Boom

I didn't really pray, except to throw up a few 'hail Mary passes' when I was really desperate or on behalf of a friend who asked. I didn't expect God to be involved in the day-to-day of my life. He was a supreme being, after all, busy looking after the whole of heaven and earth. So, this idea of giving my burdens and worry to God to carry was a foreign idea to me.

As we talked, though, I agreed to give this a try. I was desperate, so what would it hurt? But, how to even get started? And how long would this take to work?

> *"It is not enough for the believer to begin to pray, nor to pray correctly; nor is it enough to continue for a time to pray. We must patiently, believingly continue in prayer until we obtain an answer." – George Muller*

'Help' is a prayer that is always answered. ~ Anne Lamott

That day, I began to pray a simple prayer to ask God to carry my burdens for a while. I decided I would keep praying that same simple prayer every day for a few weeks to see if it did any good.

Those first days, I didn't really believe the words I was praying. I hoped God could magically fix my problems and take away the worry, but couldn't imagine how that would happen. I still believed that I needed to fix all these problems on my own.

The function of prayer is not to influence God, but rather to change the nature of the one who prays.
~ Soren Kierkegaard

As I kept praying, I began to feel a shift in my approach to prayer. From thinking an answer to this prayer was impossible to hoping God would intervene. From hope to wanting to hear an answer from God. From wanting to hear a response to believing a response was possible. From belief to anticipation; from anticipation to expectation, expecting God would actually answer my prayer; finally becoming watchful and observant to see how He would reply.

How often do we set a time-table for our prayers? "I'll pray this for a week, for 21 days, for a month." Yet, God doesn't work that way. He's not operating on our time frames or our schedules. He works in an entirely different dimension. He wants us to keep praying until the prayer is answered.

Pray until you pray. ~ Puritan advice

We need to stop asking "how long do I keep praying before I'll have an answer?" or "how long do I keep praying even though God's not answering?" Instead, we need to make sure what we're praying in in alignment with God and then commit to keep praying until we become aware of God's answer to that prayer. Keep praying until you truly believe in the prayer and can open yourself to allowing God to answer it in His way.

1. **Check your motivation.** Is what you're praying in alignment with God's plan or something for your own plan?

2. **Check your heart.** Do you believe God will really answer your prayer and are you praying with full sincerity?

3. **Check your expectations.** Do you have a preconceived expectation of how God will answer your prayer or have you opened yourself to the possibility that God may answer in an entirely unexpected way?

4. **Check your observation.** Are you looking for God's response around you? Are you being watchful and observant to see the ways God is at work answering your prayer? Are you listening for God's response or are you too busy asking?

5. **Check your gratitude.** Are you showing God your gratitude for His work in your life? Are you thanking Him for the ways He's answering your prayers? Are you cultivating that relationship with Him through regular prayer and gratitude?

Guide For Praying Deep Today:

Consider your biggest prayer request and how long you've been praying it. Are you still waiting for an answer? Review the five checks and see if your request is aligned with God. Spend some time thinking about how God may already be answering your prayer. Then, commit to continuing in prayer and PRAY!

Journal and pray your responses to the five checks:

1) Check your motivation.

2) Check your heart.

3) Check your expectations.

4) Check your observation.

5) Check your gratitude.

Close by praying Psalm 139.

_____

_____

_____

_____

_____

_____

_____

_____

_____

_____

_____

_____

Lord, make us instruments of your peace. Where there is hatred, let us sow love; where there is injury, pardon; where there is discord, union; where there is doubt, faith; where there is despair, hope; where there is darkness, light; where there is sadness, joy. Grant that we may not so much seek to be consoled as to console; to be understood as to understand; to be loved as to love. For it is in giving that we receive; it is in pardoning that we are pardoned; and it is in dying that we are born to eternal life. Amen.

(A Prayer Attributed to St. Francis, page 833, The Book of Common Prayer)

Prayer as a Life Attitude

It's down to the last minute, the final seconds of the game. What just minutes ago had looked like victory, now seems sure defeat. Too little time left, too far to go for the win. But wait, the quarterback has one more chance. He sends his receiver far down the field, all the way to the end zone. Then he lets the ball fly as far as he can throw it, hoping for a miracle.

We've all seen examples of the "Hail Mary pass" in football games or a wild half-court shot in basketball. Last ditch efforts to win the game. Most often they fail, yet some succeed and become our most celebrated victories.

The trouble with our praying is, we just do it as a means of last resort. ~Will Rogers

How often do we approach prayer with this same mentality? We're on our own, fighting to win this game of life, but only when we're desperate do we open our play books and finally choose prayer as our last-ditch, "Hail Mary pass" option because nothing else has worked.

I've done this countless times. I haven't given prayer a second thought until the needs are so great that I know I need help. "Oh yeah, let me ask for prayers for this and see if that will help." Prayer should not be a last resort, though, it's meant to be how we develop a regular relationship with God.

Don't pray when it rains if you don't pray when the sun shines. ~Satchel Paige

I'm not saying God won't listen to these desperate prayers, but I think He'd prefer us to come to Him more regularly in prayer. Not just bring Him what we're unable to solve on our own, but bring Him our everything. Celebrate the good, give thanks for everything, share the struggles both big and small.

When you grow up and leave home, do you only call your parents when you're in trouble or in need of money? Or, do you call and visit with them, share what's happening in your life, ask about what's happening in theirs? While your parents are probably always grateful to hear your voice and willing to help, they'd prefer if you called more often and just visited from time to time.

Prayer is not merely an occasional impulse to which we respond when we are in trouble: prayer is a life attitude. ~Walter A. Mueller

Prayer is meant to be an integral part of our lives, our way to cultivate a relationship with God. Yes, prayer is there for us when we're in trouble, when we're desperate, when we have no where else to turn. But couldn't it be so much more? Maybe we wouldn't even hit those depths if we were in more regular prayer?

Try using prayer as relationship building with God. If you more often find yourself going to prayer when you're in need, as your last resort, then let me suggest you try praying something different for a while. Focus your prayers on saying "thank you" for all the blessings in your life, praising God for who He is, praying the names of God and letting those promises wash over you, asking God to speak to your heart. See if this helps instill a new form of prayer in your heart and a new attitude toward prayer.

Guide For Praying Deep Today:

Take time today to just listen for God's word. Let Him speak to your heart about how you're doing at building a deeper relationship with Him through prayer and how you're doing at integrating prayer into your daily life. Listen for where He wants your prayers to focus or how He is already at work answering the prayers you've been praying for so long.

Today, spend a full 15 minutes in silent listening prayer. Yes, that's a long time, but stretch yourself. Set a timer so you aren't tempted to keep checking the clock. Clear your thoughts and just "be" with God, listening for His voice in your heart.

To prepare yourself for this time of silence and listening, try this simple breathing exercise to relax your body and clear your mind:

- Get comfortable.
- Begin breathing full breaths, in and out.
- Take a breath in. On the exhale count 50.
- As you inhale, count down to 49, then 48 as you exhale.
- Continue to count backward on each inhale and exhale until you reach 20.
- After 20, only count on the exhales. Count down to 0 and then just breathe and relax.

Now begin your 15 minutes of listening prayer with God.

Journal your experience and what you hear from God.

> "We tend to use prayer as a last resort, but God wants it to be our first line of defense. We pray when there's nothing else we can do, but God wants us to pray before we do anything at all. Most of us would prefer, however, to spend our time doing something that will get immediate results. We don't want to wait for God to resolve matters in His good time because His idea of 'good time' is seldom in sync with ours."
> - Oswald Chambers

_____

_____

_____

_____

_____

_____

_____

_____

_____

_____

_____

_____

_____

_____

_____

O Lord, you have taught us that without love whatever we do is worth nothing: Send your Holy Spirit and pour into our hearts your greatest gift, which is love, the true bond of peace and of all virtue, without which whoever lives is accounted dead before you. Grant this for the sake of your only Son Jesus Christ, who lives and reigns with you and the Holy Spirit, one God, now and for ever. Amen.

(A Collect for the Seventh Sunday after the Epiphany, page 216, The Book of Common Prayer)

PRAYING DEEP IN REAL LIFE

Five minutes somehow turns into 20. A quick check of Facebook and the next thing I know I've wasted nearly half an hour I had planned for something else. Or, I sit down to watch my favorite show on TV, but end up watching two or three. Not just a half hour break, but now two hours gone and it's time for bed.

Does this sound familiar? We're all so busy and the days just seem to slip away. How do we find time to add anything new, even if it's important?

As I stepped into this study on prayer, I worried how would I find the time to really dig deep and experience the prayers. I wanted to know them well before I wrote about them, yet I didn't think I could find the time to commit. I knew it would take a commitment of at least 20-30 minutes of daily prayer at least, but I typically only have a few minutes here and there for prayer (often as I'm driving). I knew I'd need a quiet place and time to focus and listen for God, yet my house is always abuzz.

How we spend our time is a reflection of our priorities

We're all busy, but how we spend our time is a matter of choice and priority. Somehow I make time to check Facebook and email regularly. I make time to catch my favorite shows on TV. So, why couldn't I make time to spend with God in prayer? Isn't He so much more important than Facebook or TV?

I had to be intentional about setting aside time for prayer, making an appointment with God. For me, it's been a half hour in the early morning, before the rest of house is awake. I carved this out of my morning writing time, but I knew starting the day with prayer would be so much more important.

139

Be purposeful about prayer to maintain God's purpose for your life.

Jesus gives us a good example of praying deep the night he prayed in the garden of Gethsemane. Here he prayed his most fervent prayers. He prayed for quite a while that night, probably several hours since we see him admonish the disciples three times for falling asleep.

What did Jesus pray about for so long? I'm sure he covered a lot with God that night, but the point of that night's prayer was to accept God's will as his own.

> *"My Father, if it is possible, may this cup be taken from me.*
> *Yet not as I will, but as you will." (Matthew 26:39)*

Isn't that what our prayers should be too? Even when we bring our requests to God, the request really is to bring our hearts in line with God's plans around each of those requests and to help us be open to His answers.

> *"Watch and pray so that you will not fall into temptation.*
> *The spirit is willing, but the flesh is weak." (Matthew 26:41)*

We also learn from Jesus why it's so important we stay grounded in prayer and continue to pray deep. As much as we want to follow Jesus and live according to God's will, it's hard and we're faced with temptations every day. We need to stay in prayer to help us be focused on God's purpose for our lives.

What can "Praying Deep" look like in real life?

As we conclude these 21 days of prayer, I thought I'd share a glimpse of how I've been using these prayers. I discovered I pray better when I use a variety of methods. These different experiences, and utilizing different senses and thought patterns, keep me more engaged and listening for God's word in fresh ways.

I like praying from the week's lectionary scriptures, so I'll often start the week by looking up the verses and reading through them. It gives me a chance to pray through the scriptures before I hear them in church, which I've found enhances my Sunday morning experience.

Some mornings I'll write prayers from the scriptures or journal what I'm hearing from God through the verses.

Another morning I may decide to pray through doodles or color a mandala. This is one of my favorites. I may write out a verse from the day before, phrase by phrase, committing its words to my heart. Or I may write out my prayer requests and spend time praying over each of them.

Maybe the following morning I'll walk the labyrinth. I have one printed on paper to do a virtual walk. I trace the path with my finger and allow God to speak to my heart.

Some mornings I'll just sit with my prayer request list and pray over each name and each need.

No matter the method I choose for my daily prayer, I'll always pray over the names on my prayer request list and then usually close with a prayer from the Book of Common Prayer. I have a selection of them printed as prayer cards and I'll rotate through them.

Through this discipline of prayer and exploring different ways to pray, I've transformed my view of prayer and grown my relationship with God. I look forward to my morning prayer time and often find my 20-30 minutes aren't enough and I want more. I find that prayer has become intertwined throughout the rest of my day, a part of who I am.

GUIDE FOR PRAYING DEEP TODAY:

Today, think about how you'll incorporate a deeper focus on prayer in your life beyond these 21 days. Which prayer methods did you find most meaningful? What are some practical ways you can continue to carve out more time for prayer in your day?

My challenge to you is this: How will you be intentional and choose time for God? What time will you commit for a regular appointment with God?

Your prayer time will look different than mine. It may be at a different time of day, for more or less time, with different choices for prayer methods. If you'll be intentional, though, and commit to pray deeper, I think you'll also find a renewed relationship with God and a deeper love of prayer.

Write a letter to God today and share with Him what these 21 days of prayer have meant to you and how you feel changed in your relationship with Him and in your experience of prayer. Write how you want to continue building that relationship with Him, how you will set aside more time for prayer in your week, and how you've found new ways to connect with Him.

_____

_____

_____

_____

_____

_____

_____

_____

_____

_____
_____
_____
_____
_____
_____
_____
_____
_____
_____
_____
_____
_____
_____

O God of peace, who has taught us that in returning and rest we shall be saved, in quietness and in confidence shall be our strength: By the might of your Spirit life us, we pray, to your presence, where we may be still and know that you are God; through Jesus Christ our Lord. Amen.

(A Prayer for Quiet Confidence, page 832, The Book of Common Prayer)

ABOUT THE AUTHOR

Kathryn Shirey is a writer, a mom, and a fellow traveler on this journey of faith. Kathryn had something awesome happen when she asked God for guidance on where He wanted her to serve. He didn't answer as she expected, but that sent her on a journey of discovery.

She's not sure where God's taking her or what it will mean to "go to work for God", but she is committed to finding out!

Kathryn writes about prayer, growing closer to God, and God's vision for our lives on her blog, Finding Hope (www.kathrynshirey.com).

Connect with Kathryn online:
- Blog: www.kathrynshirey.com
- Facebook: www.facebook.com/FindingHopeKathryn
- Twitter: @KathrynPShirey
- Pinterest: www.pinterest.com/kpshirey

ALSO IN THE "PRAY DEEP" SERIES:

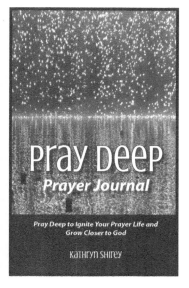

The perfect companion to the *Pray Deep* series of guided prayers. Use the prayer methods introduced in *Pray Deep* and create your own prayer experiences.

Journal Your Prayers and God's Responses

This prayer journal includes:

- 30 days of prayer journal pages, with lined pages to capture your key scripture, your prayer, and God's response.
- Pages to track prayer requests and keep those you're praying for top-of-mind.
- Descriptions of each prayer method introduced in the *Pray Deep* series to use as reference in your prayer time.

Printed in December 2022
by Rotomail Italia S.p.A., Vignate (MI) - Italy